▣ READERS

Level 3

Spacebusters: The Race to
  the Moon
Beastly Tales
Shark Attack!
Titanic
Invaders from Outer Space
Movie Magic
Plants Bite Back!
Time Traveler
Bermuda Triangle
Tiger Tales
Aladdin

Heidi
Zeppelin: The Age of the
  Airship
Spies
Terror on the Amazon
Disasters at Sea
The Story of Anne Frank
Extreme Sports
Spiders' Secrets
The Big Dinosaur Dig
The Story of Chocolate
LEGO: Mission to the Arctic

Level 4

Days of the Knights
Volcanoes and Other Natural
  Disasters
Secrets of the Mummies
Pirates: Raiders of the High Seas
Horse Heroes
Trojan Horse
Micro Monsters
Going for Gold!
Extreme Machines
Flying Ace: The Story of Amelia
  Earhart
Robin Hood
Black Beauty
Free at Last! The Story of
  Martin Luther King, Jr.
Joan of Arc
Welcome to The Globe! The
  Story of Shakespeare's Theater
Spooky Spinechillers
Antarctic Adventure
Space Station
Atlantis: The Lost City?
Dinosaur Detectives
Danger on the Mountain: Scaling
  the World's Highest Peaks
Crime Busters
The Story of Muhammad Ali
First Flight: The Story of the
  Wright Brothers
D-day Landings: The Story of
  the Allied Invasion

Solo Sailing
LEGO: Race for Survival
WCW: Going for Goldberg
WCW: Feel the Sting
WCW: Fit for the Title
WCW: Finishing Moves
JLA: Batman's Guide to Crime
  and Detection
JLA: Superman's Guide to
  the Universe
JLA: Aquaman's Guide to
  the Oceans
JLA: Wonder Woman's Book
  of Myths
JLA: Green Lantern's Book
  of Inventions
The Story of the X-Men: How it
  all Began
Creating the X-Men: How Comic
  Books Come to Life
Spider-Man's Amazing Powers
The Story of Spider-Man
The Incredible Hulk's Book
  of Strength
The Story of the Incredible Hulk
Transformers Armada:
  The Awakening
Transformers Armada: The Quest
Transformers Armada:
  The Unicron Battles
Transformers Armada:
  The Uprising

A Note to Parents and Teachers

DK READERS is a compelling program for beginning readers, designed in conjunction with leading literacy experts.

Beautiful illustrations and superb full-color photographs combine with engaging, easy-to-read stories to offer a fresh approach to each subject in the series. Each DK READER is guaranteed to capture a child's interest while developing his or her reading skills, general knowledge, and love of reading.

The five levels of DK READERS are aimed at different reading abilities, enabling you to choose the books that are exactly right for your child:

Pre-level 1 – Learning to read
Level 1 – Beginning to read
Level 2 – Beginning to read alone
Level 3 – Reading alone
Level 4 – Proficient readers

The "normal" age at which a child begins to read can be anywhere from three to eight years old, so these levels are only a general guideline.

No matter which level you select, you can be sure that you are helping your child learn to read, then read to learn!

LONDON, NEW YORK,
MUNICH, MELBOURNE, AND DELHI

Created by Tall Tree Ltd
For DK
Editor Laura Gilbert
Production Claire Pearson
DTP/Designer Dean Scholey
Picture Researcher Marie Ortu
Picture Library Kate Ledwith
Cover art by Mike Wieringo and José Marzan, Jr.

First American Edition, 2005
Published in the United States by
DK Publishing, Inc.
375 Hudson Street
New York, New York 10014

05 06 07 08 10 9 8 7 6 5 4 3 2 1

Library of Congress Cataloging-in-Publication Data

Hibbert, Clare.
The Flash's book of speed / written by Clare Hibbert.-- 1st American ed.
p. cm. -- (Dk readers. Level 4)
Includes index.
ISBN 0-7566-1014-1 (plc) -- ISBN 0-7566-1015-X (pb)
1. Speed--Juvenile literature. I. Title. II. Dorling Kindersley readers. 4,
Proficient readers.
QC127.4.H53 2005
531'.112--dc22
                    2004017129

Color reproduction by Media Development and Printing Ltd, UK
Printed and bound in China by L Rex Printing Co., Ltd.

The publisher would like to thank the following for their kind permission
to reproduce their images:
Position key: c=center; b=bottom; l=left; r=right; t=top
7 Alamy Images: Ralph Wetmore (t); 8-9 DK Images: NASA (b);
10-11 DK Images: Kenneth Lilly; 14-15 DK Images: Jerry Young;
24-25 DK Images: Chris Grigg/Keither Harmer; 26-27 Rex Features:
Charles M. Ommanney (COY / KMLA); 29 DK Images: Demetrio
Carrasco (b); 30-31 Corbis: Rick Doyle (c); 32-33 DK Images: Richard
Leeney (b); 34-35 DK Images: Richard Leeney (c); 37 DK Images:
NASA (b); 38-39 DK Images: Raymond Turvey; 40-41 Science Photo
Library: Tony & Daphne Hallas (c); 42 DK Images: EADS Astrium (b);
45 Alamy Images: Popperfoto (bl); 47 Rex Features: Novastock (SKC) b.
All other photographs © Dorling Kindersley.
For further information see: www.dkimages.com

**Dorling Kindersley would like to thank the following artists for their
contribution to this book:** Marlo Alquiza, Brian Apthorp, Brandon
Badeaux, Darryl Banks, Hilary Barta, Brian Bolland, Greg Brooks, Joe
Brozowski, Sal Buscema, Jim Calfiore, Sergio Cariello, John Cassaday,
Dave Cockrum, Dan Davis, John Dell, Pamela Eckland, Wayne Faucher,
John Floyd, Kerry Gammill, Brian Garvey, Frank Giacoia, Joe Giella, Dick
Giordano, Doug Hazlewood, Phil Hester, Josh Hood, Carmine Infantino,
Chris Ivy, Dennis Janke, Oscar Jimenez, Phil Jimenez, Gil Kane, Scott
Kolins, Joe Kubert, Greg LaRocque, Jim Lee, Ron Lim, Livesay, Kenny
Martinez, Jose Marzan, Mark McKenna, Jesus Merino, Pop Mhan, Tom
Morgan, Todd Nauck, Carlos Pacheco, Yanick Pacquette, Dan Panosian,
Ande Parks, Bruce Patterson, Paul Pelletier, Andrew Pepoy, Howard
Porter, Mark Prudeau, Humberto Ramos, Roger Richardson, Roger
Robinson, Denis Rodier, Anibal Rodriguez, Vince Russell, Scott Shaw,
Bob Smith, Ray Snyder, Mike Wieringo, Scott Williams, and Pete Woods.

Discover more at
www.dk.com

Contents

DK Readers

PROFICIENT
4
READERS

JLA

THE FLASH'S BOOK OF
SPEED

Written by Clare Hibbert

DK

Flash I
Research scientist Jay Garrick was the first-ever Flash. He gained his amazing super-speed after breathing in radioactive fumes.

Flash II
Police chemist Barry Allen, who lived in Central City, was the second Flash. He was also a founding member of the JLA.

Champion speedster

I'm the Flash, also known as the Scarlet Speedster because of my cool costume! There have been different Flashes over the years, but we all share certain things in common. Firstly, of course, we are all capable of superhuman speeds! We gain our power from the Speed Force— a mysterious realm at the far reaches of the Universe. We use our speed for good, helping to fight crime and injustice wherever we find it. That is why we teamed up with other super heroes, such as Batman and Superman, to form the Justice League of America (JLA).

This book is all about the fastest things on planet Earth—and beyond! You'll also find out lots about me, my fellow speedsters, my friends in the JLA, and my enemies.

The most famous Flash was Barry Allen's nephew, Wally West. He became Flash III after Barry's death. He is in the main picture, speeding through the skies.

Flash IV
A new hero took over as the Flash after Wally West disappeared. He turned out to be 27th-century speedster John Fox, who had traveled back in time.

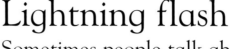

Lightning flash

Sometimes people talk about things happening "as quick as lightning." That is because a bolt of lightning can flash across the sky in a split second.

Lightning bolt
Barry Allen became the second Flash after he was struck by a bolt of lightning.

Kid Flash
Wally West was also struck by lightning. It happened when he was in his uncle's lab – and he became Kid Flash.

Thunderstorms are made up of thunder and lightning. They develop inside cumulonimbus clouds. Inside the clouds, raindrops and ice crystals smash into each other, building up positive and negative electrical charges. Electricity flows between the charges, creating a lightning flash that heats the surrounding air until it is five times as hot as the surface of the Sun! The noise that the hot air makes is thunder.

You can figure out how far away a thunderstorm is because the light travels faster than sound.

Lightning vision
Like the Flash, David Hersh the preacher was struck by lightning. He discovered that he could become immortal (live forever) by sacrificing the lives of others, and took the name Cicada.

That means you see the lightning before you hear the thunder, even though they happen at the same time. Count the seconds between the flash and the thunder to find out how far you are from the storm. Divide the number by five to get the distance in miles.

The Weather Wizard is one of the Rogues, a band of baddies who hate the Flash. The Weather Wizard uses his Weather Wand to summon up any kind of storm.

Wild winds

The very fastest winds on the planet are found inside a tornado, or twister. Tornadoes are spinning columns of air that reach down from a thundercloud and touch the ground. They spin at speeds of up to 300 mph (480 km/h).

A tornado is like an enormous vacuum cleaner. Its funnel of air sucks up everything in its path, from houses to trains. Tornadoes can happen anywhere in the world, but so many happen in the American Midwest that the area is known as "Tornado Alley." The wind speeds in hurricanes are not as fast as those found in tornadoes.

Even so, these violent tropical storms contain winds that can blow at more than 75 mph (120 km/h). Hurricanes form over warm seas. As the storm races over the water, the winds whip up freak giant waves. These can be big enough to wash away a whole city if the storm hits the coast.

Police work
Like the Flash, Detective Fred Chyre helps to protect Keystone City. He has adopted and raised Josh Jackam, the son of murdered fellow officer Julie. The Weather Wizard recently learned that Josh was actually his son and had inherited some powers of the Weather Wand.

This swirling mass of cloud is a roaring hurricane. The center of the storm is called the eye.

Fastest animals

The fastest land animal is the sleek-bodied cheetah. It bolts across African grasslands at up to 60 mph (95 km/h). Unlike other cats, the cheetah has blunt, straight claws, like a dog, that cannot be fully retracted (pulled in). These give the cheetah extra grip when it is running down gazelle and other prey. Cheetahs can sprint only for short bursts. The average chase covers just 183 yd (170 m).

The sailfish can swim even faster than a cheetah runs. It has a powerful body that can propel it through the water at speeds of up to 68 mph (109 km/h). This makes it the fastest creature in the oceans.

Cheetah
Flash's JLA teammate Wonder Woman has battled the ferocious Cheetah. The first Cheetah was Priscilla Rich, a woman who suffered from a split personality after she became jealous of Wonder Woman.

However, birds can outpace both land and sea animals. The spine-tailed swift, for instance, can fly at speeds of 106 mph (170 km/h). The fastest animal of all, however, is the peregrine falcon. When this bird of prey swoops down on its target from a great height, it can reach speeds of more than 124 mph (200 km/h), making it the fastest creature on the planet.

Fastback
Timmy Joe Terrapin is from Earth C. Superman, who often raced against the Flash, visited Earth C in a parallel universe. After he was hit by a meteorite, Timmy gained super-speed and became known as Fastback.

The speedy cheetah stalks (closely follows) its prey first, then starts to sprint toward it from about 100 ft (30 m) away.

Animal athletes

Watching animals pushing themselves to the limit makes thrilling sports, especially when they achieve high speeds. The best thoroughbred racehorses can gallop along at nearly 43 mph (70 km/h), while the fastest greyhounds—desperate to catch the racetrack's mechanical rabbit—can reach top speeds of just over 40 mph (65 km/h)!

The world's most famous dogsled race is the yearly Iditarod Trail in Alaska. The record time to complete the 1,120-mile (1,800-km) race is a little over nine days.

Superdog
The special powers of Superman's canine companion, Krypto, include speed, strength, X-ray vision, and the power of flight.

The race celebrates the dog teams that carried life-saving medicine between the towns of Anchorage and Nome. The medicine was needed due to an outbreak of the throat disease diphtheria in 1925.

The sport of racing pigeons began in the 1800s. Races can take place over hundreds or thousands of miles, and the bird that covers the distance in the fastest time is the winner. Some racing pigeons can fly at average speeds of more than 90 mph (145 km/h)!

Grodd
The evil Grodd is part of a clan of super-smart gorillas who live in the hidden Gorilla City. He has clashed many times with the Scarlet Speedster.

Dogsleds are pulled by teams of huskies. With their thick fur and sturdy build, the dogs can cope with extremely low temperatures.

Slow down
As slow as a land turtle, Turtle Man used a ray gun that stole the Flash's powers and gave them to his men. The more the Flash tried to run, the faster the bad guys went.

Planting evil
Poison Ivy can affect how quickly plants grow—and she uses them for her evil plans.

Slow living

Not everything lives at a breakneck speed. The snail is so famous for living life in the slow lane that people even talk about "crawling at a snail's pace." It would take a snail a whole minute just to slither the length of your hand.

The tortoise is also known for its leisurely pace. It does not need to run because its tough, horned shell protects it from harm.

The tree sloth moves very slowly along a jungle branch.

The tree sloth wins the prize for being the laziest animal, snoozing all day and most of the night. It moves so little that algae grows on its hairy body! Even its digestive system is slow—it can take a week to digest a meal.

Of course, plants hardly seem to move at all. The slowest-growing is a fruit tree called the dioon. It grows just 0.02 inches (0.77 mm) in a year.

Chronos
Archvillain Chronos was able to slow down time, freezing people on the spot. He developed his time-altering powers when he was in prison.

Human speedsters

Athletes are the closest humans have to speed heroes. The first person to run 1 mile (1.6 km) in less than four minutes was Britain's Roger Bannister in 1954. Since then, speeds have kept improving, thanks to more time spent training and the development of high-performance running shoes. Today's sprinters can top 25 mph (40 km/h) over short distances!

The fastest swimming stroke is the front crawl. The best swimmers can swim at 5 mph (8 km/h) on average.

Surfing is a much faster way to zoom through water, or rather over it, because it harnesses the power of a breaking wave.

Snowboarding is similar to surfing, but faster because the boarders speed across a snowy, slippery hillside. It is still not as popular or as fast as skiing, though. The fastest skiing speeds—achieved over special speed trials—are a mega 150 mph (240 km/h) or more. The best cross-country skiers can only manage average speeds of around 16 mph (25 km/h).

Human reactions

Every human being is a champion speedster—on the inside!
The human body is made to react to its changing surroundings faster than the blink of an eye. The brain can trigger movements without us being aware of any thought process.

The quick responses our bodies make to danger are called reflexes. When a nerve ending senses pain, for example, it sends a message to the nearest part of the spinal cord.

At once, a signal travels back to the body part, making it jerk away from the source of the pain. Doctors can test the speed of our reflexes by tapping just below the kneecap—this should make the knee jerk!

Nerve cells carry their speedy signals in the form of tiny bursts of electricity. The electricity leaps from cell to cell along junctions called synapses in less than one-thousandth of a second.

Blue baddy
Evil Cobalt Blue attacked Sela Allen, daughter of the Flash from the 23rd century. He slowed down her nervous system so that no messages could travel from her brain to her muscles. This meant she was paralyzed.

A sprinter cannot leave the blocks until 0.1 seconds after the gun has fired. This is the fastest time it takes for the body to react to the sound of the gun—any quicker and it is a false start.

Fast weapons

In any kind of combat, from one-to-one fighting to full-scale war, a fast weapon gives its owner the edge. People have used bows and arrows for over 30,000 years.

A modern longbow arrow can whizz along at 344 mph (550 km/h).

A cruise missile is a type of weapon that can guide itself to a target.

A *Tomahawk* cruise missile flies through the air at speeds of 550 mph (880 km/h). It is hard to detect because its engine gives off so little heat. The next generation of missiles, planned for 2015, will be even faster, flying at 3,600 mph (5,760 km/h)! That's a little faster than a speeding bullet.

Quivering champ
Green Arrow Oliver Queen uses his amazing skill with a bow to save members of the JLA. He fires special, customized arrows, some of which pack a high-explosive punch.

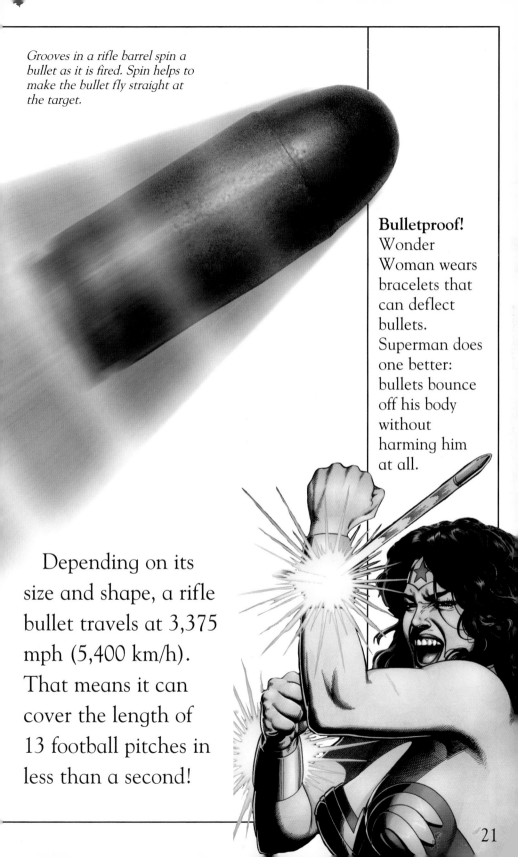

Grooves in a rifle barrel spin a bullet as it is fired. Spin helps to make the bullet fly straight at the target.

Bulletproof! Wonder Woman wears bracelets that can deflect bullets. Superman does one better: bullets bounce off his body without harming him at all.

Depending on its size and shape, a rifle bullet travels at 3,375 mph (5,400 km/h). That means it can cover the length of 13 football pitches in less than a second!

Terrific two-wheelers

A cycling champ can pedal along at nearly 55 mph (90 km/h)—or even faster if he or she slipstreams behind another vehicle. With lightweight frames and a streamlined shape, today's racing bikes are designed to create less drag and more speed.

The quickest way to travel on two wheels is by motorcycle. Racers are the fastest, some topping 186 mph (300 km/h)—as fast as a high-speed train!

Vanishing point
While the Flash was chasing an evil lookalike called the Rival (above), the villain went faster than the speed of light—and vanished into thin air. He had hit terminal velocity and found the Speed Force!

Off-road motorcycles are slower, because they're built to take part in tough, cross-country racing.

Motorcycle racing is a very popular sport. Speedway racing is for lightweight motorcycles on a racetrack. The most famous speedway event is held each March at Daytona, Florida.

Long-distance speedsters prefer the grueling Paris-Dakar rally, a 7,000-mile (11,265-km) race that is open to cars and trucks as well as bikes. Part of the course is through very hot desert, so it's no wonder that competitors try to finish the race as quickly as possible!

Power source
The Speed Force is an energy field that exists beyond the speed of light. Max Mercury (above), the Flash's friend, discovered that all speedsters drew their powers from this mysterious energy field.

23

Four wheels

Dark Knight's charger
With its lightweight metal frame and 1,500-horsepower engine, the Batmobile has a cruising speed of 225 mph (360 km/h). It can even reach 350 mph (565 km/h) for short bursts, thanks to its powerful jet afterburner.

Car racing has been a sport almost since the invention of the engine. The first big car race, or Grand Prix, took place in 1895 in France, when the winning car averaged a speed of about 15 mph (24 km/h)!

Modern racing cars are a lot faster than that!

Formula One Grand Prix racing cars are only allowed small engines, but they can still reach speeds of more than 160 mph (260 km/h). In other races, such as the Daytona Busch Clash, normal cars are "souped up" and raced at speeds of 200 mph (320 km/h).

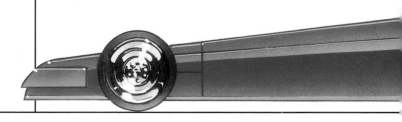

Dragsters are the fastest wheel-driven cars of all. They have huge engines on tiny, slender frames, with small wheels at the front and huge tires at the back. The huge rear tires give the dragsters as much grip as possible. Dragsters are raced on a straight strip and they can zoom to speeds of over 300 mph (500 km/h). They even have to use parachutes to slow them to a halt!

Passing
After he was struck by lightning, Barry Allen wasn't aware of his new powers at first. The first he knew was when he ran for a cab—and passed it!

Some dragsters increase their speed so quickly that they have a bar at the back to stop them from flipping over.

Supercars

To go faster than a dragster, a vehicle has to be very streamlined to cut through the air surrounding its body. Record breakers have to use rockets or jet engines. *The Blue Flame* was a rocket-powered car that reached 635 mph (1,016 km/h) in 1970.

Traveling at close to the speed of sound in a car is risky. The ground has to be smooth, since the slightest bump could flip the car and destroy it —and its driver.

Rogue machine
Young Tony Gambi agreed to help the Rogues defeat the new Flash. They put him inside a machine called the Humanifold in order to create a super rogue.

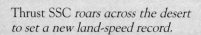

Thrust SSC *roars across the desert to set a new land-speed record.*

Land-speed record breakers use natural flat surfaces, such as the Bonneville Salt Flats, Utah, to race their machines against the clock.

Jet-propelled cars are the fastest cars in the world. The land-speed record was set in a car called *Thrust SSC*, which used two supersonic-fighter jet engines to generate about 110,000 horsepower! It was the first car to travel faster than the speed of sound, setting a speed record of 768 mph (1,228 km/h) in 1997.

Transformation
Record breakers add jet engines to improve their cars. The Humanifold bonded the Rogues' weapons to Tony's body, creating the Ultimate Rogue. They called him Replicant!

Fast track

Hometown
Apart from being home to the Flash, Keystone City is famous for its speedy train network. It is linked to Central City by a huge iron and steel bridge. The Flash assembled the bridge after a villain called Blacksmith demolished the old one.

Trains have always been symbols of rapid scientific progress. The first trains reached speeds of 25 mph (40 km/h), which some people believed would be too fast for the human body to survive! Modern high-speed trains reach ten times that speed, perfectly safely. The fastest train is the French TGV—"TGV" stands for the French words *Train à Grand Vitesse*, meaning "High-Speed Train." The TGV reached an incredible 322 mph (515 km/h) in special test runs in 1990, though it normally works at about 150 mph (240 km/h). The Japanese Bullet Train's normal speed is even greater, averaging speeds of 171 mph (273 km/h).

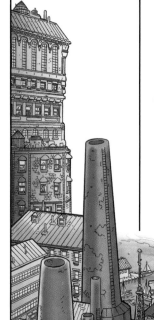

The Japanese rail service is testing a new train. It has reached speeds of 345 mph (552 km/h). Seconds after leaving the station, the train's wheels retract, and the train "flies" above the track on a cushion of magnetic fields.

Tornado Twins Born in the 30th century, Dawn and Donald Allen inherited speed from their father, Barry Allen. They fought crime in secret, disguised as tornadoes!

The Japanese Bullet Train's curved nose is based on the streamlined shape of an aircraft.

Water speedsters

Speed through the water is measured in knots, from an old technique for measuring a ship's speed by feeding out a rope with knots tied in it. Knots measure speed across nautical miles, and one knot equals 1.15 mph (1.85 km/h).

It's hard to be speedy over water. Water is thicker and heavier than air, so it drags on vessels and slows things down.

When he wants to swim even faster, Aquaman hitches a ride on the back of a killer whale.

Walking on water
Crossing a body of water holds no problems for the Scarlet Speedster. He runs so fast that he can just zip across the surface.

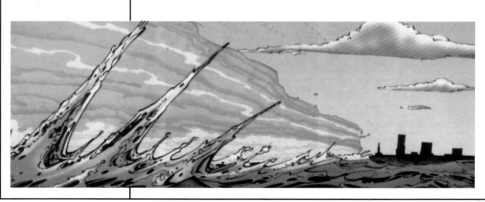

The fastest watercraft contact the water as little as possible. The *Decavitator* is a strange water speedster—it has no engine! It uses an air propeller, powered by a "cyclist" in a streamlined cockpit. In 1991 it reached a speed of 18.5 knots, or 21 mph (34 km/h). Motorized water racers can go much faster—a waterbike can manage 56 knots, or 65 mph (104 km/h). Hydroplanes are fastest of all because they skip along the surface of the water. In 1978, a hydroplane called the *Spirit of Australia* reached a record-breaking speed of 276 knots, or 317 mph (511 km/h).

Johnny Quick
Crime-fighter Johnny Quick knows a secret formula that connects him to the Speed Force. It is based on a sacred mantra found inside the tomb of an Egyptian pharaoh.

Johnny Quick was an All-Star Squadron hero during World War II.

High fliers

The fastest record breakers break away from the surface of the Earth. Many jet planes break the sound barrier, which means they travel faster than the speed of sound. At ground level, the sound barrier lies at 760 mph (1,216 km/h). High above the Earth, where the air is thinner, the sound barrier is broken at 650 mph (1,040 km/h).

When a vehicle breaks the sound barrier, it travels faster than its own noise. Noise piles up behind it to form a shockwave, which is heard on the ground as a bang, or "sonic boom."

The first aircraft to break the sound barrier was a Bell X-1, flown by Chuck Yeager in 1947.

Quick flight
Although she cannot achieve the speeds of the Flash, Jesse Quick has mastered how to go fast enough to take off!

The X-series of aircraft have been record breakers ever since. An unmanned X-43A aircraft broke all records in 2004. It reached a speed seven times faster than the speed of sound, at 4,780 mph (7,648 km/h).

Ring of light
Green Lantern's ring can shape light into solid forms instantly, creating anything that the wearer imagines, such as a protective shield.

This is one of three X-1 supersonic planes built in the 1940s. The "X" stood for "experimental."

Jets and rockets

Jet engines struggle to "breathe" at the highest speeds. It is easier to use rocket engines to push beyond the records achieved by the X-43A. Rockets do not have to collect oxygen from the air they are traveling through to burn their fuel—everything they need for thrust is carried in tanks.

Sonic boom
The Pied Piper used special sonic (sound) weapons against the Flash. Like his namesake, he also enchanted people with his flute-playing.

The US X-15 rocket plane was lifted to a high altitude (height) by an enormous B-52 bomber. Once there, it dropped off the bomber's wing and fired its own rocket engine. This took it so high and fast that its test pilots were counted as "astronauts" by the US Air Force!

One of them, Neil Armstrong, later joined NASA and became the first man to walk on the Moon. The X-15 reached 4,520 mph (7,322 km/h). Only space rockets have ever carried human beings faster than this.

The X-15 flew at nearly seven times the speed of sound!

Racy robots
In the 27th century, a breed of speedy robots was developed to serve with the police force. The Speed Metal robots help the new Flash to track down criminals.

The Speed Metal robots are equipped with time-traveling devices so that they can track and chase criminals through time.

Blastoff!

You have to go pretty fast to escape the pull of Earth's gravity. The speed needed to overcome gravity and escape into outer space is called "escape velocity." From Earth, escape velocity is about 25,000 mph (40,200 km/h).

The US space agency NASA built the gigantic Saturn V rockets to push Moon missions clear of the Earth. Each rocket stood 364 ft (111 m) tall, and weighed nearly 3,000 tons (3 million kg). Most of this weight was the fuel needed to power the rocket.

Earth's atmosphere is thin near space, but there are still enough gas particles to create heat through friction. Anything moving through air at high speed heats up. When astronauts return to Earth, they hit the atmosphere at nearly 20,000 mph (32,000 km/h).

All change
The Flash's costume can withstand the heat produced by high-speed travel and its outer layer of Teflon minimizes air resistance!

The Flash's costume fits inside a custom-built ring. When the ring is released, gases in the air fill the suit so that it can expand to full size.

Air friction acts as a
brake to slow the craft
down. The underside
of the spacecraft is
coated with high-
tech fireproofing materials—so it does
not burn up like a shooting star.

Rocket boots
Honorary JLA
member Steel
cannot fly—but
he does have a
pair of jet
boots! These
allow him to
rocket up into
the air.

*The Saturn V rocket
blasts clear of the
launchpad. It was
the largest rocket
NASA ever used
and carried people
to the Moon and the
Skylab space station
into orbit in the
1960s and 1970s.*

Speed in space

JLA satellite
For a while, the Justice League of America's headquarters was a satellite in orbit above the Earth. Later, the League built the Watchtower on the Moon.

Speed in space is hard to measure, because everything is moving—there is no fixed point to measure against. By using the Sun as a point to measure from, however, we know that the planets of the Solar System loop around the Sun at incredible speeds.

The Earth's orbit around the Sun takes precisely one year—that's what a year measures! Each second, the Earth moves nearly 19 miles (30 km).

Comets are also part of the Solar System and produce a long glowing tail as they get near the Sun.

Green man
J'onn J'onzz, the Martian Manhunter, is one of the most committed members of the JLA. His special powers include telepathy (being able to read people's minds), shape-shifting, and the ability to reach great speeds.

The Martian Manhunter can also fly and has the ability to make himself intangible so that objects pass right through him!

That's a speed of 67,052 mph (107,283 km/h)!

Some of the other planets of the Solar System are even faster. Mercury, tucked in close to the surface of the Sun, zooms around it in a circuit at nearly 108,000 mph (172,800 km/h). Mercury's orbit takes just 88 Earth-days to complete, compared to Earth's 365.

Distant Pluto plods along at a mere 10,800 mph (17,280 km/h), and takes nearly 250 years to complete one lap around the Sun.

Black Flash
The Black Flash is the form that Death takes when it comes for speedsters. It was seen before the deaths of Barry Allen and Johnny Quick.

Distant speedsters

Even the Sun, known in astronomy as Sol, is speeding along. It is moving in a huge circuit around the center of our galaxy, the Milky Way. Astronomers think this lap takes Sol about 226 million years to complete. That might seem lazy, but only because it is such an enormous distance to travel—the Sun is zooming along at about 486,000 mph (777,600 km/h)!

Galaxies move, too. The nearest galaxy to the Milky Way is called Andromeda. It is too far away to measure the distance in miles or kilometers. Instead, we use light-years—the distance a beam of light can travel in one year.

Andromeda is 2.2 million light-years from the Milky Way. However, we are approaching it at a speed of about 312,500 mph (500,000 km/h). At this rate, the two galaxies will collide in 3.5 billion years.

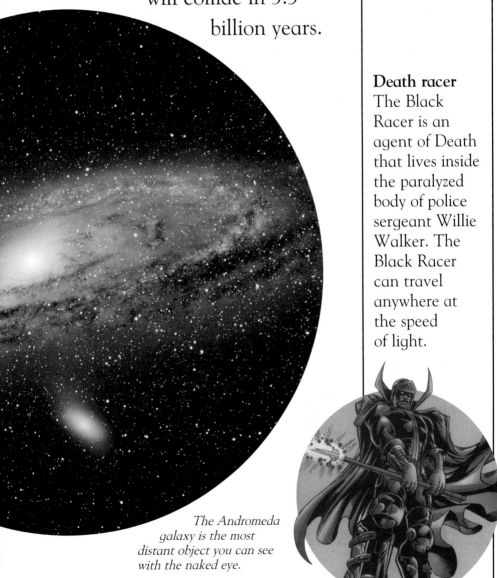

The Andromeda galaxy is the most distant object you can see with the naked eye.

Death racer
The Black Racer is an agent of Death that lives inside the paralyzed body of police sergeant Willie Walker. The Black Racer can travel anywhere at the speed of light.

Zippy data

The speed of light is used to measure the big distances of deep space because it is the fastest thing known to science. Light travels at about 186,500 miles (300,000 km) per second, or 625 million mph (1,000 million km/h).

Brain drain
The spare space in the Flash's brain was taken over by an alien probe from the giant starfish-shaped alien Starro (above). Batman freed Wally West from Starro's clutches, and the Flash speedily destroyed the evil alien's computer.

This soldier's field telephone transmits data by satellite dish.

People use light speeds to transfer data around the world. We can send a beam of light along an optical fiber, and use a detector at the other end to decode the signal very rapidly. Light speed applies to many types of energy rays, not just the light waves that are visible to human eyes. The radio signals that bounce via a satellite around the curve of the Earth are also traveling at light speed.

Electrons inside computers and ordinary wire cables travel slightly slower than light. However, even these signals are far quicker than the messages that flash along our nerves and through our bodies.

Bat computer
In the shadows of the Batcave sits the most advanced computer in the world. It provides Batman with all the information he needs to fight crime.

Strange forces

The speed of light has a special place in the way that science understands the Universe. It appears in the most famous physics equation of all time, $E=mc^2$, part of Albert Einstein's Theory of Relativity. The "E" in this equation stands for energy, "m" for mass, and "c" for the speed of light.

Light always travels at a certain speed in space. This is a breathtaking 625 million mph (1,000 million km/h). This knowledge gives scientists useful clues to the basic rules of physics. It is also handy for astronomers, helping them to understand what they see through their telescopes.

Einstein's theory also shows how space, time, and gravity make up one fabric, obeying clear mathematical rules.

Do not fold! Working on one of Einstein's unfinished theories, the evil scientist Edwin Gauss discovered the secrets of inter-dimensional travel. He became the Folded Man!

For normal objects, the faster they travel, the more energy they need to accelerate. This makes it impossible for anything other than energy rays to travel at the speed of light.

German-American physicist Albert Einstein lived from 1879 to 1955. In 1921, he was awarded the Nobel Prize for Physics.

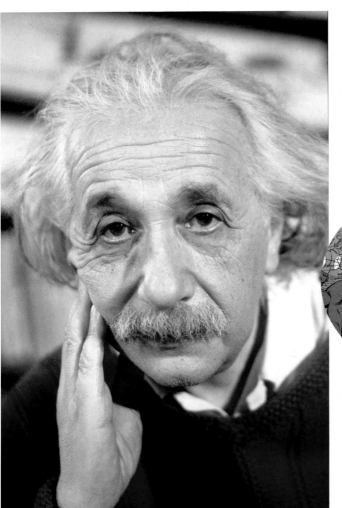

Stealing time
Evil scientist T.O. Morrow invented a fourth-dimensional grapple machine to steal inventions from the future.

Good vibrations
The Flash is able to vibrate so fast that he can move through solid objects.

VREEEEEEEEE

The Cosmic Treadmill
Barry Allen developed a treadmill that could launch him back or forward in time, when he ran on it at top speed. The Cosmic Treadmill also allowed him to reach parallel universes.

After Barry's death, the Cosmic Treadmill became an exhibit in Keystone's famous Flash Museum.

Beyond light speed?

Even traveling at the speed of light, reaching other stars would take tens or even thousands of years. So there are good reasons to look for quicker ways to travel.

Some scientists are looking into particles that can travel faster than light. These imagined particles are called tachyons. We are a long way from creating tachyon spaceships, however. First, we need to invent experiments to test whether tachyons even exist.

Another possibility is that we might discover shortcuts through space, or wormholes. If they existed, wormholes would be very small and exist for only a fraction of a second. We would need to discover how to make them bigger and last longer.

A third idea could be to bend or "warp" space, bringing distant points closer together. This is how some spaceships travel in movies. Warp engines might be possible in theory, but they would need more fuel than exists in the whole Universe!

Professor Zoom
The Reverse-Flash used the Cosmic Treadmill to time-travel into the past and fight the Flash.

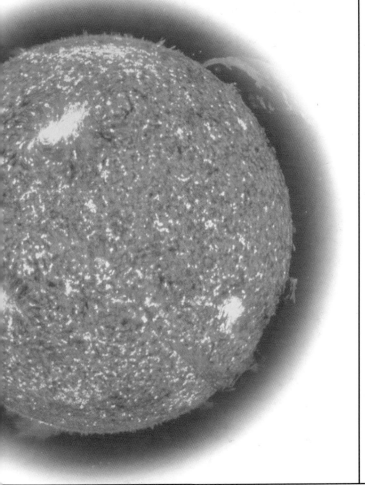

Space is so huge that traveling to other stars, similar to our Sun, would take millions of years using the rockets we have today.

Glossary

algae
Simple living things that, like plants, make food from sunlight; unlike plants, algae do not have roots, stems, and leaves.

atmosphere
The layer of gases around a planet or moon.

comet
A lump of ice and rock flying through space. When it passes near the Sun, it has glowing tails of dust and gas.

cumulonimbus
A tall cloud which often has a flat top and a dark bottom. It is usually linked with storms.

drag
The resistance created as an object passes through air and water. This force slows objects down.

escape velocity
The speed at which a spacecraft needs to travel to break free of Earth's gravity.

friction
A force of resistance caused when one object rubs against another—for example when a vehicle rubs against air particles.

galaxy
A body made up of millions of stars, as well as gas and dust.

gravity
The pulling force that operates between any two objects that have mass. It is the force that pulls your body toward the center of the Earth, keeping your feet on the ground.

horsepower (hp)
A way of measuring the power of an engine, by comparing it to the power of a horse.

hydroplane
A type of motorboat that skims along the surface of the water at very high speeds. It even raises its hull completely out of the water.

insignia
A badge or emblem. The Flash's insignia is a yellow lightning flash on a white background which he wears on his red uniform.

light-year
The distance that light can travel in one year – around 5.9 million million miles (9.5 million million km).

mantra
The words that make up a sacred chant.

meteorite
A fragment of space rock that has fallen onto a planet or moon.

optical fiber
A glass cable used to transmit pictures, sound, and other data, by means of light waves.

orbit
The path of one object around another more massive object in space.

parallel universe
Another universe that exists alongside our own. There is no evidence that parallel universes exist.

radioactive
Describes a material that gives off high-energy rays, some of which may be harmful.

satellite
Any object held in orbit around another object by its gravity. These include artificial satellites and moons.

shaman
A medicine man or the religious leader of a tribe.

slipstream
A stream of air which flows behind a moving vehicle. This stream has lower wind resistance and can be used by another vehicle traveling behind to move more easily.

Solar System
Everything held by the Sun's gravity, including the planets and comets.

Index